D1552630

ISBN: #97986930099493

You Are Not Your Problem

Jill Raiguel, MS, MFT

Drawings by Kris Hofmann

Dedication

Dear Reader,

　　This book is dedicated to my parents who could transform the everyday into play. Dad floated flowers in the toilet on birthdays. Mom played music to dust by on the piano to inspire us to do chores. As a result, I love to learn, especially if it's fun. I designed this book to not only make you smile but to help you see yourself, your friends, and family. Kris's drawings gave my story, that I wrote thirty years ago, charm and character and made it easy even for children to understand. I hope it helps you untangle yourself while it brings a smile to your lips.

In joy,

Jill Raiguel, MS, MFT
jillraiguel@gmail.com

Acknowledgments

Special thanks to Tommy Raiguel and Linda Lysakowski, ACFRE, who worked tirelessly on the layout of this book.

"Jilli-e-e-e-e!" Anne called out my name in her happy, uplifting voice, and I felt happy. My problems... dropped away, and I was all right once again.

When I heard that friendly accepting voice, I stepped out from under my problems.

I was suddenly bigger than my latest argument with Tom. But what did Anne have?

What was in that magical voice that made me feel so good? So one day I asked her,

"Why do I always feel better after I talk to you?" I said.

Anne smiled. I knew she knew something I didn't know. Her eyes twinkled.

"I could tell you I have a special magic but I don't."

"But you have mag...." I exclaimed.

"No, YOU do!" she insisted.

"Me?"

"Yes, you!" Anne was so sure of herself.

I couldn't understand what on earth she was talking about. I called Anne whenever I needed a boost. I always felt better after our talks, but I never thought about why. I just knew it did. Today was the first time I asked, "How come?"

"Anne, you make me feel good," I said.

"No, I don't," she threw the words back at me. "You make yourself feel good... or bad," she began.

"Well, let's back up a minute. I don't do anything special to make you feel good. I just know who you are. You are a person bigger than any problem you might be facing, and when you call me you feel like:

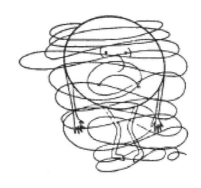

"...you're smaller than your problem. You're overwhelmed. I simply remind you of that:"

"...you are a big person who is capable."

"Now," Anne continued, "if I were interested in keeping you small and dependent on me, I'd let you think you needed to keep talking to me:

"...to unravel yourself from your problems. You don't. You can do it yourself, like a self-cleaning oven."

This I WAS curious about, I revered my dear friend, Anne, as if she had a potion she used for chasing the blues away. She was up all the time.

And people loved to be around her. When she did have a problem, she faced it and solved it.

"Please teach me!" I begged.

"I'll help you teach yourself," she said. "But you'll have to give up somehting. You'll have to give up feeling sorry for yourself, getting all the sympathy."

I hated to admit it, but she was right.

"I guess that's true," I said.

"Good, you are willing to look at yourself. But first remember you are not your problem. At times you may feel like you are drowning:

...but you have the power to shift how you hold your situtation."

4

"See, I call it a situation or a challenge, not a problem. Remember, when my car exploded on the Golden Gate Bridge? Pretty terrible right? Well, I just got out of the car and said to myself, 'This is where the new car comes in.' I thumbed a ride to the gas station, got the car towed, then went out and bought a used car with the insurance money. I saw the inconvenience as an opportunity in the predicament immediately. I've trained myself to be:

...not:"

I found myself arguing, "But I'm not you, I couldn't do that. You come from a family of positive thinkers. I'm just not that optimistic."

Anne didn't give up, "I disagree. You have all the stuff to learn this. I'm not talking about a skill or trait, I'm talking about the ability to shift how you see a situation. Take when Tom broke up with you..."

"Yes, it took a year to recover from that!"

She continued, "Because he wounded you, right?"

"But he did! He just stopped calling," I declared.

"Maybe," Anne said gently, "I mean he did stop calling, but you think that meant something bad about you."

"What?" I was a little confused.

"Well, like: Did you think you were bad? Or you did something wrong? Or you were wrong?" She explained.

"Of course!" I had felt all those things.

"And you felt you weren't good enough as a person," Anne added.

"Of course!" I said.

"Well, I have another point of view. Instead of thinking you were crushed:

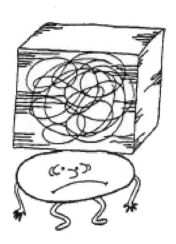

"...maybe he just stopped calling you because he got scared. And you are fine. in fact, I think you're a 10!" she stated absolutely.

Amazed, I said, "You mean you always saw me as a 10, even when I was crying my eyes out?"

"Always!" Anne simply said.

"In fact," she continued, "You are pretty paralyzed when you feel crushed. When you can seprate from your problem, you feel powerful again; like you can solve it. The problem doesn't go away, but you are in a better position to handle it."

"I see." I didn't know exactly what to do with this news. Anne seemed to read my mind.

"Just sit with all this. There'll probably be a situation very soon where you'll have a chance to practice."

She hung up. I was so deep in thought, I didn't even say thank you.

The next day I was walking to work my usual way. It was raining so I had my umbrella up, but no raincoat. The gutters still overflowed from the night's heavy downpour. Just as I stepped off the curb a car rounded the corner and splashed muddy water all over me. I was soaked; my dress ruined. The car pulled over. A well-dressed man burst out of the driver's door shouting apologies:

"I'm so sorry! I'm so sorry! You were right there... and your dress."

Without hesitating I said, "I'd like you to have my dress cleaned."

This man I didn't even know reached in his wallet and pulled out his card:

Then he wrote a note on the card and handed it to me, "Come in to one of my dry cleaners, and we'll clean your dress free of charge."

He got back into his dark expensive car and drove off. I was soaked but elated. I sprinted the last ten blocks to work, and stopped at the ladies room to wash off my legs and shoes. As I walked in the corridor, my boss, took one look at me and said,

"What happened to you?"

"A splash attack from a Lincoln Continental."

We both laughed.

"But the good news is he offered to clean it." I waved his card triumphantly.

"Great! Take your break early and go downstairs to the A-1 Cleaners on the corner."

I quickly changed into my gym clothes and was out of the building in a flash. I left my muddy rags at the cleaners and was working at my desk by 9:45 am. And... I was beaming.

Betsy, who sat across from me, glared straight at me:

"Well, you're looking very cocky!"

"You wouldn't believe this morning!"

And I told her the freeze-dried version.

"And... I'm taking us to lunch," I said.

"You're on," Betsy replied.

About thirty minutes later Betsy blurted out, "You're not upset!" She was telling me AND asking at the same time.

"No, I feel great!" I answered.

"What happened?" Betsy asked. "Stuff like this usually strings you out for days. At least you'd be crying."

Only then did I notice something was missing, or maybe something was new. I wasn't sure.

Betsy continued to prod, "What happened to you? I don't mean about the jerk splashing you. I mean what happened to you on the inside!"

The changes on the inside, those were harder to explain. But I had to try; Betsy and I had been friends for a long time.

"I guess it began when I was talking to Anne..."

"Yeah, that's the gal who's so disgustingly happy," she glowered. Betsy was going to be a tough customer; she could be very negative. But I plowed ahead.

"Yeah, but I found out why. Or better, what she does, not to make herself happy but to get out from under her problems:

"...so she can solve them and go on."

"OK, I'm interested," Betsy said reluctantly.

"Well, Anne told me about not being your problem," I started.

"What?" Betsy asked.

"Yes..."

"Is this going to be one of those spiritual conversations?" as she folded her arms across her chest. "I think I'll be sick right now."

"Betsy!" I was shouting but I got her attention.
While she sat silently, I tore off a sheet of paper and simply drew:

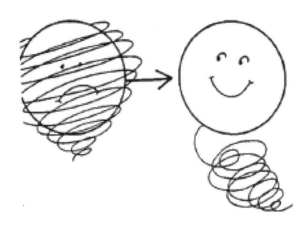

...and started back to work.

Betsy said nothing, until lunchtime, which was extremely unusual for Betsy. At 12:15 we both walked to our favorite restuarant for birthday, holiday, and retirements, too expensive for everyday, but this wasn't everyday. I let her begin.

"What is...?" and she drew:

...on her napkin.

"You are not your problem," she mimicked me.

"Well, that's the secret Anne told me."

"So!" Betsy stared at me like she meant 'big deal!'

"Well, when I got splattered this morning, I could have been upset."

..."I could have let the situation get to me. But I saw that I could turn it into an opportunity. In fact, I did that so fast I didn't even get upset."

Chomping on her crab salad, Betsy continued, "Well, lunch is nice, and you got your dress cleaned., but I don't see... Well, you were just in a good mood when that guy splashed you."

"No!" This was going to be tougher than I has thought. Betsy and I had worked together for years. We had coffee together, lunched together, commiserated together. After I listened to her complaints about Ralph; she'd be all ears for mine about Tom. I felt sorry for her, then she'd feel sorry for me. Maybe feeling sorry for yourself was part of why people get so stuck in:

...and can't get to:

As I slogged ahead talking to Betsy, I suddenly appreciated Anne's many talks with me. I'd been really stuck in:

"Betsy, you know your relationship with Ralph."

"Yeah!"

"Well, I think you mostly feel like you're in it," I took a big risk and said, "like a victim."

"I am! He'll call for a date and never show up. He can be so loving and sweet and then he disappears for a month." Betsy looked like a whipped puppy.

I'd heard this all before. My on-again off-again Tom was just like her Ralph. We were both women who put up with men who treated us terribly. I shuddered to think I'd be a victim just like Betsy was being now. Maybe that's why she was making me so mad. I could hear the irritation in my voice as I said,

"Betsy, you are doing just what I did. I felt powerless and at the mercy of Tom, the crumb."

She continued her plea, "But I love Ralph and he loves me. I know he does. He just didn't treat me very good. It's not his fault."

She tolerated this jerk. Now I was really mad, "Well whose fault is it?" I questioned.

"Mine I guess. I just don't think I can find anyone else. And, at least I have a boyfriend to talk about even if he treats me badly."

I wanted to tell her she was crazy, but I restrained myself. I ordered coffee so I could buy time to think of what to say next. I prayed to the silver coffee pot as the waiter poured: "I'm stuck. Please give me something intelligent to say here." After a moment I took out my note pad and drew:

"Betsy, you are my dear friend, and I love you. You may think this sounds harsh but I'm saying this because I want to help you." I corrected myself, "I want you to help yourself."

Betsy continued, "I know. We've always helped each other."

"I don't think so, I think we've felt sorry for each other. We've given each other sympathy; but maybe we never solved anything."

Now Betsy was mad: "Maybe I don't want anything solved. Maybe I like it the way it is!"

"My point exactly. I think you love your problems:

"I think you're attached to having a crummy relationship and feeling sorry for yourself."

And, I quickly added so she wouldn't punch me, "And I think I have been a victim too. I loved talking about how horrible Tom was with you and getting all your sympathy.

"But nothing changed. I still have Tom, the crumb. And you have Ralph, the jerk."

I was having one horrifying insight after another as my words tumbled out... and Betsy was still listening.

"What's worse is you and I have based our whole relationship on 'I'll feel sorry for you, if you feel sorry for me'."

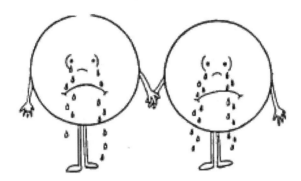

I was fast discovering I was sick to death of it. I hated Betsy's sob story almost as much as I hated my own. As I brought my thoughts back to the table, Betsy was ordering a slice of banana cream pie and complaining:

"I will never lose weight!"

I bit my tongue. I couldn't blast her again for being the victim. She would really punch me. Something told me she would have her own insights just like I was having. Seeing myself in Betsy, I had a little compassion for her. A gentle feeling settled over me.

"Betsy, I relished our ain't-it-awful talks, but I haven't been very happy. I haven't been much fun to be with. I hate being with myself. I want to be happy, I want to... NO! I am happy! I am fun!"

I said it boldly, really for myself. That meant making some changes, but I felt strong and ready to leave Tom. Betsy wasn't listening; or even looking at me. Her eyes were looking at something far away. I decided to leave her in her thoughts, but I touched her sleeve slightly.

"It's time to go back to work."

I don't think she could have answered with words, instead she got up from the table. I guided her through the tables and back to work.

After that lunch Betsy and I stopped having coffee or lunch together. I had a hard time being around her awfulizing. It was as it we moved our friendship from 20 inches away to 20 yards away from each other without saying a word. Maybe I could be her friend in the future, but not right now.

I found myself gravitating toward a woman named Audrey. Audrey was happily married and had two kids. She spoke cheerfully about her life. I liked being around her. As the weather warmed up, we'd take our lunch to the nearby park and enjoy the pink spring blossoms.

One day Audrey said, "You know, I enjoy you so much! You're happy and bright and turned on to life."

"Well, I wouldn't go that far," I tried to deny it.

"Yes, you are!" as if she needed to convince me. "Even my husband says so, and he's Mr. Moody."

"Well, thank you! But I have to say I feel the same way about you."

Audrey continued, "You must come from a very up-beat family."

I laughed, "Oh no, this is a very recent change. I'm not happy 24 hours a day, but I'm not down in the dumps for months at a time. I used to be... well:

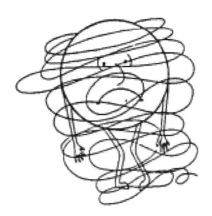

"I couldn't really solve anything when I felt entangled, when I felt my problem was bigger than me."

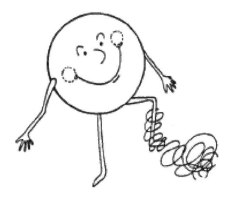

"When I'm able to shift how I hold my problem, I can begin to find solutions."

Audrey beamed, "Exactly! You put it so precisely! I've been trying to convince my husband of that for years. but he still insists on worrying 24 hours a day. At this point, his worry is such an old friend, I don't think he'd know what to do without it."

I boldly drew:

And I said, " You mean he loves his worries like an old bathrobe that should be thrown out."

"Well, not exactly." Audrey was noodling around in her head for just what she meant.

"It's more like:"

"He thinks his troubles are a part of him. When I go and try and take them away or even brush them aside...:"

"...he feels, well, like I'm taking away a part of him."

I simply said, "Oh, he thinks his problem is a part of who he is. And nothing gets resolved because he thinks it's a part of himself. He doesn't think it's a problem."

"Yes, exactly. I even yelled at him once, 'You'd feel naked without your big important PRO...BLEMS.'

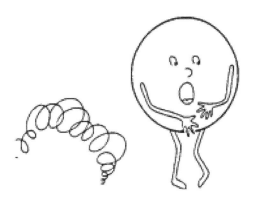

"Boy, I was angry!" Audrey shared. "Of course, I was right, but he sulked for days to punish me."

I was learning that Audrey had a hard time being around George just like I had trouble being with Betsy, and George liked his worries just like Betsy liked being a victim.

I inquired, "What do you do when he sulks. I have a friend... She's so victim-ey, I can't spend time with her anymore."

Audrey replied, "In some cases I think you have to let go of negative people. But I'm not ready to throw out my husband. I leave him alone for a few days. Then he'll walk up behind me while I'm washing dishes at this kitchen sink and hug me from behind. He knows I love that. And we've made up. But nothing's changed; it'll happen again. i feel so cheated!"

"What do you mean cheated?" I asked.

"When George and I were first married, we skipped down the street. Even though we were poor students, we were Mr. and Mrs. Joyful. We had problems, but we felt we could handle whatever life threw at us."

"We giggled over pouring each other's morning coffee," she continued. "We read each other stories at night. He'd send me a picture postcard from his office that said, 'Wish you were here!'" Her eyes filled with tears, "That was 15 years ago!"

I didn't know what to say, but my hand naturally wanted to reach out and rest on hers.

Her hand instinctively squeezed mine as if that helped. Finally, I was able to say, "I'm sorry I lost my best friend. I mean we used to be friends and..."

"I know you can't stand her now!" Audrey finished my thought.

"Yes! And I miss her. Not her PROBL...EMS, but the fun we had. I'd forgotten the movies and our beach trips until you talked about George."

Audrey said, "Your mascara is running down your cheeks," as she handed me a tissue. Not until then did I notice I was crying too. I laughed and she dabbed her eyes.

She composed herself, "I can't just leave George; we have too many good things, two beautiful children for starters."

Suddenly, it was important to help my friend. I mean really help her. I clutched my soggy tissues in my hand and thought: 'Let me know how to help this person!'

I found myself saying, "Have you ever told George what you've just told me?"

"No!" she volleyed back.

I somehow knew I should pause. In a moment she continued, "I guess I could. If he gets mad or sulks that's no worse than it is now!"

"And tell him you love him, and that you want the old in-love days back." I was surprised at how smart that sounded.

Audrey grinned, "I'll try, I'll try it tonight... You know, you're good at this."

"What?"

"Helping people!" she concluded.

I smiled at Audrey but at myself, too, because I realized I had to talk to Betsy. I was a little scared, but what was more important, my fear or my old friendship with Betsy?

Monday morning I found Audrey sitting in the staff lounge half-smiling from behind her coffee mug. I could hardly wait to hear the report.

"Well?" I began.

"Well, it went OK."

"Just OK?" I prodded.

"Yeah, he listened. After my speech, he said he'd like that too."

"Great! And what else?" I urged

Audrey went on, "Then we watched an old movie. He held my hand. And I made popcorn with real butter. We hadn't popped popcorn for years."

"That's wonderful!" I was delighted with her success.

"Yeah, but he wasn't much fun!"

"Give it time. You have to let talks like that sink in. And when you're asking people to change, they may need to noodle around about for a while."

"Noodling! You're so smart about people!" Audrey stated.

I didn't feel smart, but I was saying smart things lately. Just then Betsy walked in and handed Audrey a postcard.

"This is for you. It came in the mail overnight," Betsy said.

Audrey read her picture postcard silently, and her eyes puddled up. She handed it to me. It read: 'Wish you were here! - Your George.'

I couldn't chicken out now. I caught up with Betsy as she was walking back to her desk,

"Wanna have lunch?" I asked cautiously.

"Yeah! OK," Betsy said flatly.

"...In the park?"

"Good! I'll order sandwiches from Joe's," she said like a robot.

"Fine," and I walked to my desk.

It was a start.

At 12:15 Betsy and I walked to Joe's, our favorite deli. Joe greeted us.

"Haven't seen you girls in months!"

It had been months since we'd ordered Joe's pastrami on rye. It had been weeks since we'd had lunch together. Joe handed us our order.

"Thanks," I was nervous about being too positive.

In the park I couldn't avoid the issue any longer.

"I miss you," I began.

26

"I miss you too," Betsy thawed slightly.

"I miss our after work picnics at the beach. We had so much fun! ...But, I don't miss..."

She cut me off, "I know that, too!"

We ate in silence. Then I ventured, "How's Ralph?"

"The same," she went back to her robot response.

I was sorry to hear that. I think she knew I didn't want to hear more. I saw clearly that Betsy did not want to give up Ralph or feeling like a victim. That's what Anne meant when she said you'd have to give up something. She wasn't ready to give up feeling sorry for herself.

Betsy did ask, "How's Tom?"

"I haven't seen him in some time. I wasn't willing to put up with how he treated me any more. I'm worth more than that!" I hoped I was getting through to her.

"Oh!" Betsy said as if I'd said something dreadful.

Changing the subject I said, "The flowering plums are splendid!"

"They're OK, I guess!"

She couldn't even enjoy the April flowers. I felt sorry for her and sad for myself. I no longer had anything in common with Betsy; but, I wasn't angry at her.

I merely said, "Are you ready to head back?"

"Yeah!" She picked at the peeling paint on the park bench.

As we walked I wanted to reach out, but I didn't want to encourage her gloom-and-doom. How could I let her know: I like you but I don't like the way you act? How could I be friends when she was so wedded to her negative attitude?

Maybe being a good friend means having to move away from her for a while. She looked like she had a black cloud:

...that followed her everywhere. She thought life was mostly cloudy; and I was seeing life get mostly sunny. At least I was feeling like I could get out from under the clouds faster.

I feel sad or angry or afraid from time to time; I still have problems. But I asked myself; what action can I take to solve this? And more important, I felt capable to take action and not vegetate under the weight of my problems.

On Friday I caught Audrey skipping down the hall. She even tried to tickle me at the copy machine. I didn't have to ask, although she told me.

"George and I..."

"I know, you're glowing. Your face tells the story," I smiled.

"Thanks. And thanks for knowing just what I needed to do," Audrey said.

"I didn't," I said.

"Yes, you did. George and I want you to come to dinner. Meet the kids. See our family in action. 7 pm OK?"

"OK, what can I bring?" I asked.

"Yourself!" Audrey said.

I rang Audrey and George's doorbell. As the chimes were finishing, George opened the door. He struggled to keep his balance as two boisterous kids, obviously Sally and Max, tugged at Dad's legs.

"Kids, meet Jill. Jill, this is Sally and Max."

Max was already riding his trike down the hall, and Sally was playing shy behind Daddy.

"Hi!" I said, and Sally ran into the kitchen just as Audrey came out.

"Welcome to our crazy house," Audrey beamed.

We hugged.

After dinner and an enthusiastic dose of Sally and Max, we adults took our coffee to the family room. While the fire warmed our faces, I learned more about Audrey's George:

"You know, dinner is only a small way we have to repay you," George began.

"Repay me?" I asked.

"You transformed our marriage," he announced.

"No, you transformed yourselves," I answered.

To Audrey, "You're right, she is modest."

"No, I just want to be accurate. You really transformed it yourself," I corrected him.

George continued, "You gave us... I mean Audrey, the notion and she brought it home. I hate to admit it, but you helped us. I wanted to do it all by myself. That's the macho in me. I thought I didn't need anyone telling me what to do... But when I saw the sadness in Audrey's eyes," He looked at her lovingly, "I finally had to do something, and I was ready. I know I'd been moody:"

"I thought that's the way a husband was supposed to be. Isn't a man supposed to be serious and responsible... a good provider on top of every little and big problem that comes along... I remember finger painting in peanut butter when I was five. That was the last time I was really silly."

We all three laughed. Audrey had a mouthful of coffee and spit it out all over herself.

As we mopped up Audrey, George continued, "My dad was Mr. Serious:"

"He was a responisble father and husband. He carried his job, his worries, and his problems with him always."

"He wasn't much fun either, and without thinking I'd become my father. I thought when you grow up you can't have fun."

Audrey piped in, "I'd better lock up the peanut butter now!"

He tickled her, then said, "My dad had ulcers and couldn't sleep nights. Looking back I think his problems made him sick."

I said, "Probably, after a while he was no longer wearing his problems:"

"He took them inside and they made him sick."

I elaborated, "Actually, his thinking made him sick. If he'd only known that he could have left his worries at the office:"

Audrey chimed in, "George, you know you haven't taken any sleeping pills since we've been... well, more playful again."

Mildly startled, George said, "That's right! And I haven't had any aspirin either. I feel terrific! I was well on my was to an ulcer. I think Dad's:

"...was so familiar to me, I didn't know any other way. I thought that was the way I was forever and ever."

Audrey said, "That sounds fatal."

George said, "I certainly felt like it was."

I said, "I realized I haven't had a cold... well, since I broke up with Tom."

Audrey, "That drip!"

"Now, there's a guy that carried around his problems," she added.

I wanted to defend him but I knew she was right. I continued, "And I worried about him all the time. Did he love me? What did I do wrong? Was I good enough? How could I fix myself so he'd love me? No wonder I was sick all the time. I didn't realize I deserved better. I was a mess!"

"No," I corrected myself, "I thought I was a mess. and that fit nicely with Tom's view of himself."

Audrey smiled, "The drip and the blob! That perfect couple!"

"Frightening, isn't it"

Audrey said, "Unfortunately, I think lots of couples and friends are like that."

I continued, "And I don't think they know any better.:'

George said, "I didn't. And it seems so simple now. You're not your problem!"

"The things that happen to you are not who you are."

I said, "Now we're all sounding like my friend Anne. I think she'd like that."

Audrey said, "You should teach this."

"What?"

"Your ideas," she said.

"They're not mine," I argued.

"But you explain them so simply, people should know about them," she insisted.

George commented, "I agree. That's a great idea!"

Audrey jumped in with, "You could run a class at the church."

"I couldn't charge," I said.

"Well, give a free evening," Audrey had a ready solution.

"OK, I'll think about it."

I drove home full of good food, friends, and ideas. The next day I had a call to Anne.

"Anne, I have this problem." I was beaming.

"Hi, Jill-e-e-e!! What's up?"

"I have no problem!"

"Wonderful! I'm thrilled! What are you going to do with all your free time?" She was playful, but serious. I didn't realize until then that being your problem, wearing your problem, having coffee over your problem takes a lot of time.

37

"Well, I'm going to teach a class,"I said.

"Great! On what?" Anne asked.

"I'm going to talk about my cartoons. I have these little drawings about how we hold our problems. I don't know if anyone will come, but I'll be there."

Anne said, "I'm very proud of you!"

"Thanks. And thanks for hanging in there with me."

"You bet," Anne replied.

"I invited Betsy but she doesn't want to come. She hates me because I'm so happy now."

Anne suggested, "Maybe she's just not ready yet, you never know."

"Right! I'd love you to see me up there... And I'd love to see you in the front row."

"I'll be there in spirit."

"I love you," I said. "You're such a great friend. In fact, this has opened up a whole new way to be friends... A friendship based on being whole and happy... What a concept!"

Anne replied, "I love you too." We hung up the phone.

That was the first time I'd called Anne already filled with what I'd call her magic potion. I'd filled myself, and I was cleaning out my problems faster and faster... like a self-cleaing oven.

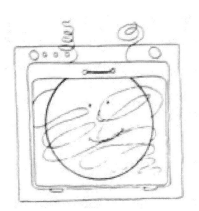

Smiling inside, I flew through the next weeks. Audrey and George arranged for a room at the church. They called friends and so did I. Audrey baked cookies and promised to maked the coffee. George attended to chairs. They had the confidence in me I lacked. I continued rehearsing in my head. I went to bed planning, I dreamed I was drawing cartoons, I woke up answering questions in my class.

Friday night finally came. I put on my favorite flowered dress, the one I felt best in. As George and Audrey helped people find their seats, I drew on the board:

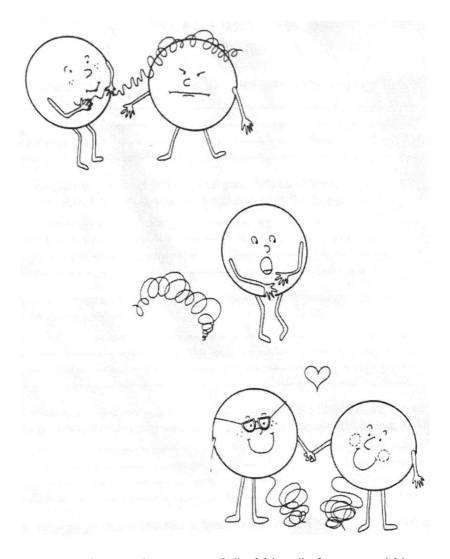

I turned around to a room full of friendly faces, and I began:

"Welcome! Thank you for coming." I took a deep breath... I was really doing this. "I'm calling my talk this evening: YOU ARE NOT YOUR PROBLEM."

I glanced at two late-comers who were finding empty chairs. Betsy and Ralph sat down in the last row.

Study Questions

1. What is your favorite drawing and why? Who does it remind you of? Write a brief story about that person.

2. Describe a time when you felt like you were your problem; by that I mean, you felt entangled in your problem.

3. Describe a time when you felt bigger than your problem.

4. Do you have a friend that you feel good around? Who? Describe what he or she does to have you feel good.

5. Describe a time when you felt under your problem. What did you do to get out from under it?

6. Who do you know who likes to complain all the time and never solve anything? Write a brief story about that person; include something you did to try to help him or her.

7. What did you learn or re-learn reading this book?

8. Can you think of a drawing that depicts a kind of person who should be in this book? Describe.